Triggers
That Cause Buyers
to Open Their Wallets

Extreme Psychological Buying Triggers
and More...

Dr. Treat Preston

TABLE OF CONTENTS

Triggers That Cause Buyers to Open Their Wallets
Extreme Psychological Buying Triggers and More...
©Copyright 2013 by Dr. Treat Preston

Introduction – For Every Gain There's a Loss; For Every Loss There's a Gain!

As a behavioral scientist for over 3-decades, my job as a research scientist is to study the human mind in all kinds of situations and conditions.

As in nature, the human mind seeks balance. Balance within the human body or physiologically is called homeostasis. Balance with the human mind is called sanity.

Mind research scientists have long sought the reasons behind the mind's ability to create success as well as turn on itself and create failure.

One of the most unique features of the human mind is that it is gullible. It is easily fooled even when the person is aware that they are being fooled, i.e. magic shows.

The human mind cannot tell the difference between fantasy and reality. Hollywood built a billion dollar industry over this fact.

This is why you cry in sad movies. Yes, your conscious mind knows you are watching a movie but your subconscious mind does not so it reacts as if the situation is real.

Next, the human mind reacts to perception first rather than reality. Perception is more important and ad executives worldwide know this fact and write their ad copy accordingly. In advertising jargon, this is called "branding".

- ❖ Psychology only studies the observable aspects of the mind and discounts the unseen or intangible aspects of the human mind.
- ❖ Behavioral science attempts to study the intangible aspects of the human mind...why you do the things you do and more importantly why you don't do what you should do.
- ❖ There is no such thing as commercial psychology versus personal psychology. The mind uses the same mechanism to evaluate all types of relationships.
- ❖ Everything we do revolves around relationships. We relate to our environment, our friends, family, co-workers, other people and even our pets. We are social animals.

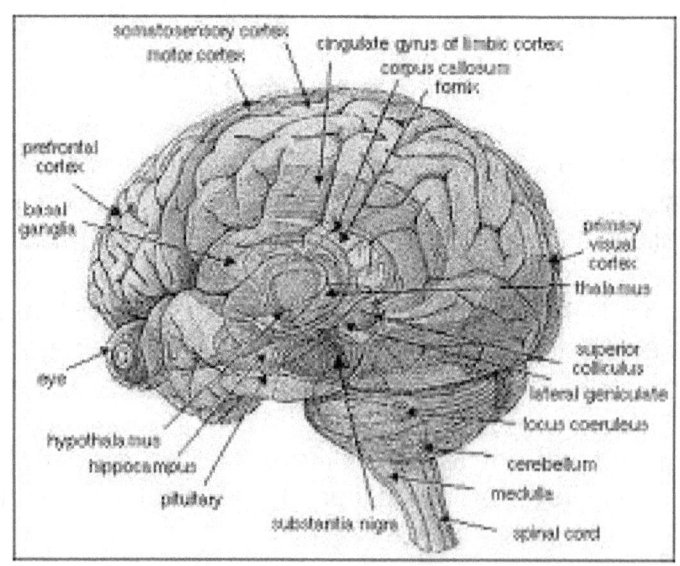

Truisms About the Human Mind

- ❖ Pain vs. Pleasure – people are more motivated to avoid pain than seek pleasure.
- ❖ A person that is suffering depression will seek relief (notice I didn't say cure) before they seek happiness.
- ❖ The human mind cannot tell the difference between fantasy and reality.
- ❖ The human mind gravitates to the desires, emotions and will of its psyche. People grave entertainment so fantasy dominates their existences.
- ❖ The human mind is easily distracted! You can either be the cause of these distractions or other stimuli will be the cause but rest assured people WILL BE distracted because the human mind is gullible.

The human mind responds quickly to these three forms of stimuli

- ❖ Sex
- ❖ Humor
- ❖ FEAR

But the greatest of them all is FEAR!

BTW – on the positive side we have faith, hope, love, but the greatest of these *is* LOVE.

Fear usually takes the form of what is called "Scarcity Thought"

You are afraid that someone will have what you feel belongs to you or that others will have more "stuff" than you.

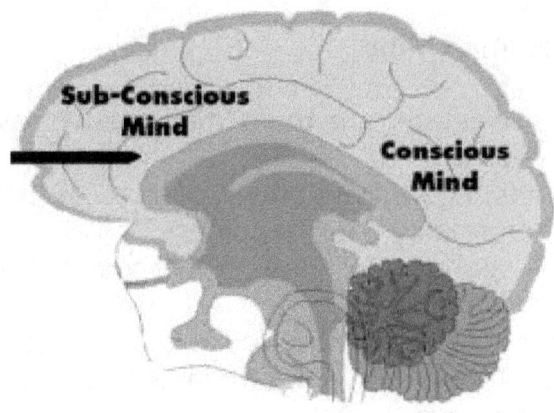

❖ The subconscious mind is often referred to as the "heart," and is the control mechanism the body uses to store our beliefs.

❖ These beliefs are stored as pictures in our "hearts" and create frequencies in our bodies.

❖ We know that the optimum human frequency is a little below 7.83 hertz. To drop below this frequency brings on the onslaught of disease. To rise above it a person demonstrates psychic abilities.

❖ Harmful beliefs that cause unhealthy frequencies are the source of almost all problems - physical, mental, emotional.

❖ The subconscious mind creates a belief system, which we call "pictures of the heart."

❖ These pictures involve either visions, or dreams/fantasies.

In this book, I want to outline different ways the mind is fooled and perceives as it pertains to ad copy that is written to 'trigger' the buying impulse. I have included both online and offline triggers. This is fascinating stuff so get ready to be wowed!

Chapter 1 – Buying Triggers

Buying

Triggers

I have a famous saying – "Tell then Sell! In other words, tell a story first that a customer can readily embrace and where the customer's mind inserts the customer into the story and you have winning sales copy!!!

Meanings lie in the feelings, not in the words. Left brain, intellectual logic and content focused words, can be totally accurate and completely wrong!

Words that ring and words that sing are words that reach the heart.

Weak and predictable words can never penetrate the, "I'm not listening barrier," that guards the heart.

Only words that create "instant pictures" have power.

When we choose words we have to ask, "What images do they create? How do these word-pictures make the person, I'm addressing, feel?"

The mind works by the ear!

Words create pictures and pictures talk back.

The inner dialogue is called thinking.

Sub-conscience thinking is the combining of sounds and preconceived images. How a person perceives this unconscious dialogue, determines "conscious decisions."

Words that sound good, go-to-work <u>immediately</u>! Getting someone's attention requires you to capture the imagination with a picture that is more appealing than the one his, or her heart is already watching. The right words are how you do it.

Revolutions create the vocabularies that drive them! Everyone who uses the words becomes a teacher.

We also have what I call positioning. Positioning is the battle for your mind to either embrace a vision, or a dream.

Positioning is not what you do with the vision, or dream; it's what you do in the heart. The easiest way to own the position in the heart is to be first!

When I teach human behavior science to salespeople, I teach them that in consumer marketing, the leading brand in any category is almost always, the first brand that has been heard.

Whoever owns the position in the heart owns the category! If you can't be first in your category, create a new category.

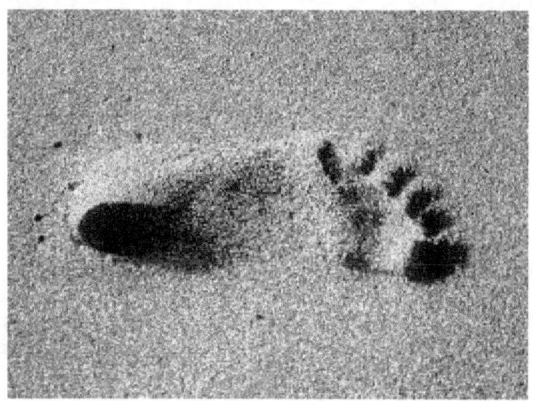

Marketing is a battle over impressions, not products. Perception is everything!!!

When you promote the category, you have no competition. The most powerful marketing concept is to own a word in a person's heart. Words that "sound good" create positive mental images, below conscious thought. Words that sound good together are powerful memory devices.

In life, the leading brand in any category is almost always the first brand that panders to the lusts of a person. As in marketing, whatever owns the first position in the heart owns the category!

The category I am speaking about in life is the MIND! If vision is not first in your category, then fantasy becomes first.

Life is a battle over perceptions, not impressions. Once again, perception is everything.

Everyone perceives FIRST to be best. Whatever you promote in the category you have no competition. If the category (mind), embraces a vision, then it is expressed first. If the category embraces fantasy, then it is expressed first.

A branding iron to the rump will work for cows; nothing external will brand the human heart.

Branding is about how our 10,000 billion brain synapses cause us to feel about a vision or a dream and by our inherent human natures we always gravitate toward the emotional side of our psyches unless trained to do otherwise.

Branding is the instantaneous evaluation and verdict of every experience, good, or bad that we have had with an emotional trigger. It's an immediate, "thumbs up, or thumbs down."

Branding is not what we consciously think and determine; it's about what our hearts feel, decide automatically, and instantaneously, when we hear, or see the trigger. If we don't feel anything, our hearts say, in effect, "Return to sender."

You must tell your target audience you were in their current position. Next, tell them how your product pulled you out of that position. For example, you could say in your ad copy, "Don't worry, I used to be just like you. I was way over my head in debt. But I decided to create a financial formula so no one else would ever go through all the pain and humiliation of bankruptcy like I did."

You must challenge your readers at the end of your ad. Make a bet with them; if your product doesn't solve their problem, offer them a free product in return. People love to gamble and most are greedy. You're just using it to your advantage so you can sell them your product or service. Some people like to gamble just because it's fun.

Questions distract the mind and cause a person to switch from what they are thinking to what you want them to think. Get your audience involved in your ad by asking them questions. They'll automatically want to answer the questions in their mind. For example, you could say in your ad copy, "Where do you want to be weight-wise in the next 5 months?" Another example, "Do you want to weigh that much or more 2 years from now?"

Be sure to introduce yourself in your ad copy. Haven't you ever read ad copy and wondered who was selling the product halfway through? It's a big turn-off. For example, you could say, "Hello my name is (your name and a little about yourself)." Another example, "It's (your name) here, I'm going to tell you about..."

Always start your ad with a story. It draws people right into your ad and they forget they're being sold to. For example, you could start your ad, "Once upon a time ..." Another example would be, "Last year, one of my friends and I were..."

Eliminate the hard-to-understand jargon on your ad copy. Unless your product calls for technical words, you want your ad to be read without people pulling out a dictionary. If you need to use a word your target audience might not under-stand, define it or use an example to help them understand it.

Be sure to create benefit intensifiers for your list of ad copy benefits. For example, the benefit: "Save More Time", the benefit's intensifier: "Never Seen Before!" You could also intensify your headline, sub-headlines, guarantees, postscripts, etc.

On technique is to have a famous and respectable person on your banner ad representing your product, website or service. People will click because they'll trust that person over you. For example, you could say, "The famous (name) has even bought our product! Click here to see why!"

You then load your ad copy up with a large amount of benefits and bonuses. People will think and feel like they are getting a lot for their money if they buy. For example, if you read an ad which had 40 benefits listed, then saw a similar one with only 10 benefits listed, and both were around the same price, which one would you buy?

And don't forget to use words that create emotion.

Everybody has emotions; people will have more interest when they are emotionally attached. Use words like mad, happy, angry, sad, excited, scared, surprised, etc. For example, "Imagine how happy you will be when you can finally afford taking that exotic cruise!"

Make sure you list any publications which have written about your business in your ad. It could be a product review, on a top ten list, an article, etc. For example, "(title) magazine says....," "(title) Times say....," "(title) news says...," etc. Another example, "(title) magazine rates our product 10 out of 10!"

"Do you want fries with that?"

You then sell more back-end products to your existing customer base. You've already created rapport and trust, and proved your credibility to them. That's why it's usually easier to sell to them the second time. Sell back-end products that relate or complement the first product you sold them.

Always make it a practice to upsell to new and existing customers. After they decide to buy one product, offer them another product at the point of purchase. You already have them in a "yes set" because they are going to buy your main product.

Always cross-promote your products and services with other businesses that aren't competition. You will reach a wider audience at less cost. The other business should have the same target audience. For example, if you're selling picture frames, you could team up with a photography studio.

Be sure to write your content so it attracts your visitors' five senses. Use plenty of adjectives. They will stay focused on your website and block out other distractions. For example, you could say, "Our product will satisfy you better than a glass of iced water on a hot day!"

Always promote yourself as well as your products. Write articles, ebooks, reports, etc. When you endorse other products for commissions, people will think your statement is extra-credible because you have established yourself as an expert.

Another good technique is to trade advertising with other businesses to save revenue. You could trade e-ezine ads, banners ads, links, print ads, etc. If the other business doesn't want to trade, offer them something extra in return. It could be extra ads, free products, commission, extra advertising time, etc.

Always tell your visitors what their friends or family will probably think when they buy your product. People care about what other people think of them. For example, you could say, "Your dad will be so happy when he sees you've bought him a new tool box!"

It is important to add low cost bonuses to your offer that have a high perceived value. It could be ebooks, Members Only sites, consulting, e-reports, etc. Make sure they are original and no-one else is giving them away.

Always create trust with your prospects by telling them something they already know is true. They'll know for sure you're not lying and begin to trust you. For example, you could say, "I know you want to increase your sales..." Another example, "I know you want something for nothing..."

Be sure to follow up with all your prospects. You can use a free e-ezine, a follow-up autoresponder, an update or reminder list, etc. You could follow up to make sure they don't have any problems or questions, and then just mention another product you are selling.

Be sure to tell your potential customers special events your business has sponsored. It could be charities, fund- raisers, charity auctions, etc. You could tell your prospects that you will donate a percentage of their order amount to charity. This could increase your profits because it might persuade them to buy more.

Always tell your potential customers about any mergers or joint ventures with other reputable organizations or businesses they would recognize. If they like or trust those businesses, it will help your profits when they know you are teamed up with them. Plus it can instantly brand your business.

Be sure to tell your potential customers some valuable information within your ad copy. This will create rapport with them. It could be tips, how-to information, case studies, etc. Also design and start your ad out like a free report or article. People will be less hesitant to read it.

Always tell your potential customers about reviews of special events your business attended. It could be trade shows, seminars or conferences. You will be informing them and selling to them at the same time. Plus if they attended the same event, and then you both have something in common which can help persuade them to buy.

Be sure to tell your potential customers stories about your customer service. It could be how you helped a new customer, an award you won, etc. For example, you could say, "The other day a woman called and wanted to know if she could get a refund, because she bought the wrong product and couldn't afford to buy the other one till she got a refund. We said, 'Of course you can' and even made her refund a top priority."

Always tell your potential customers stories about your employees. It could be about why they like to work for you, their personal profile, etc. For example, you could say, "Our Human Resource Director, Susan, said she loves working here because we are all so polite, caring and friendly."

Always tell your potential customers about the milestones and goals your business has achieved. It could be a sales goal, customers served goal, etc. For example, you could say, "Last year we answered over 100,000 customer service calls and emails, and solved every problem our prospects and customers had."

Always tell your potential customers about the innovations your business has discovered. It could be inventions, new technologies, patents, new products, etc. Your prospects and customers will be impressed that you are constantly researching new ways to make their lives better.

Be sure to tell your potential customers the things you have done to improve your product. It could be lighter, faster, heavier, slower, etc. You could show pictures of your product before and after you improved it. This tells your prospects that you care about them and that you want their experience with your product to be really good.

Be sure to tell your potential customers a little history or past information about your business. It could be how it started, how you got the product idea, etc. This kind of information helps your prospects and customers know more about the kind of business they are buying from and make it a more personal experience for them.

Testimonials

It is important to publish testimonials for your free things. It would increase their value and if they're viral marketing tools, you'll have more people giving them away. Another tip is to give testimonials for other people's freebies. They might publish it on their website. You can include a link back to your website too.

Always give your visitors a good time so they will visit your website again. Use a few jokes, humorous graphics and funny stories. You could also provide a free online game they can play on your website. If your visitors like it they will revisit again and again. Plus they might tell other people about it.

Always make your content into a story format. People will want to keep reading to find out what happens at the end of the story. For example, you could say, "On Tuesday, June 13, 1988, I was driving to work and...." Another example, "Just the other day I was at the store and..."

It is important to build rapport with your potential customers by teaching them something new. Provide them with free ebooks, articles, tips, courses, etc. Offer them a free weekly ezine. Include new, original articles, interviews with experts, case studies, website profiles, news stories, etc.

Don't forget to allow your visitors to collect things from your website so they will stop back again and again. It could be a series of software, ebooks or articles. People like to collect things because it's a goal. It makes them feel good because every time they collect a new item, they are fulfilling their goal.

It is important to keep each page of your website consistent or similar. Use similar text fonts, colors, graphics and background on every page. If you have one web page that is blue, one that is red and one that is orange, it doesn't look professional. It would look like you just threw it together and didn't think things through. Would you buy a product from someone who gave you that impression?

Always tell your readers how fast they can receive your product or service in your ad. Their buying decision may be based on how fast they can receive your product. They may need it by a certain deadline. For example, you could say, "You can download our ebook within minutes after you order."

Be sure to tell your readers they'll receive surprise bonuses. This'll raise your readers' curiosity and make them want to buy so they can find out what the surprise bonuses are. You could also not tell them and make it a real surprise. For example, imagine how you would feel if you bought a product and got a second one for free without knowing it ahead of time?

Always use attention grabbing adjectives to describe your product. For example, "Sizzling, incredible, high powered, ultramodern, killer, eye-popping", etc. For example, which sounds more appealing to you "software" or "time-saving software"? Another example, "membership site" or "top secret membership site"?

Always use a testimonial on your banner ad. This'll give people proof they aren't wasting their time clicking on your banner ad. The testimonial should include enough information so they understand the offer. You could also make them click the banner to read the testimonial. For example, "See What (famous person's name) Had To Say About Our Marketing Ebook!"

Iit is important to increase your traffic by holding free teleclasses. You can refer people to your website for more information. You can also mention things you sell at the end or during the teleclass. You could offer one daily, weekly or monthly. You could also invite other experts to speak and teach.

Be sure to tell people what they're thinking and feeling as they read your ad. Most people will actually experience the feelings. Your statements should help sell your product. For example, you could say, "As you are reading this ad, you begin to think about a life without debt."

Always ask your visitors questions that induce thoughts, feelings, memories and emotions that will influence them to buy. You could ask questions about people's future, present and past. For example, you could say, "How many times in the past have you wished you had stuck with your diet?"

Always tell your prospects that your product tastes, smells, sounds, looks, or feels better. When you target the senses, you're triggering human appeal. Your senses also send the information to your brain and subconscious mind. Your prospect may be persuaded to buy because he or she imagined how something tasted.

Be sure to create an email discussion list. The list should be related to your website's subject. Place your ad on all posts and it will remind people to visit your site. You could list your email discussion list at online email list directories. Just type in the keywords "email discussion lists" into the search engine of your choice.

It is important to prove your product is a bargain. Add a lot of freebies to your offer or, if you've sold the product for a higher price before, show them the difference. For example, you could say, "Order our product for only $19 before we raise it back up to $29! That's a huge $10 savings!"

Always make your website more useful. Sell ad space, generate hot leads, answer visitors' questions, offer free content, be news friendly, etc. There are so many things you can do to make your website more appealing and profitable. It's a good idea to regularly surf the web and study other websites for ideas.

Always make the most of each visitor. Sometimes they'll think your price is too high. You should provide a variety of similar products at different price ranges. Offer free products, free trial or sample products, low priced products, subscription products, rent products, high priced products, etc.

Always test and redesign your banner ads till you get your desired click-through rate. Once you do, join many banner exchanges and buy ad space. For example, if you achieved

10 clicks per hundred viewers then placed your banner in 30 places and got 100 viewers per day from each place that would be 9000 visitors per month!

Always use holidays as a reason to get free publicity. Write a press release or article about the current holiday. It'll have a high chance of being published. For example, your title could be, "10 Smoking Ways To Increase Your Sales On Thanksgiving Day!" Another example, "How to Turbo Boost Your Traffic on Valentine's Day!

Be sure to utilize the free content which is freely available on the Internet. Publish one article on a single webpage with your main website link then upload it as a doorway or lead page. You would then just submit it to search engines and web directories. Also place an ad for your ezine on the lead page to capture visitors' emails.

Always test your new products on the bottom of your home page or on other pages. You don't want to take away hits from your best selling products until others are proven. You could also take your new products and sell them as upsell or back-end product till they become more steady earners for you.

A good technique is to use a little humor in your ad copy. It could be the little extra push needed to close a sale. People are usually persuaded easier if they're in a good mood. How many times have you let your guard down and bought something when you were in a good mood?

Be sure to offer a free trial of your product for a set period of time. Don't charge or bill your customers until they have decided to buy it. That should remove any perceived risk for them. For example, if you gave a person a sample of your membership website and they liked it, they would probably join and pay for a full membership.

Be sure to make your sales letters or ads sound like it is common sense to buy your product. For example, you could say, "Everyone knows you can't make money..." Another example, "Everyone realizes that designing a professional website isn't hard like it use to be."

Be sure to make sure your ad copy sounds like you know what you're talking about. If people sense you don't, they won't buy. For example, you could say, "I know this product will help you achieve your goals!" Another example, "I guarantee our product will end your fear of snakes forever!"

Always allow other websites to sell your product for a percentage of each sale. They can take a percentage of the sale and send you the rest of the order to drop ship. This is one way to set up an affiliate-like program without any tracking software or technology. It works really well for products that have to be shipped.

It is important to tell your prospects that you offer a lower price than the competition. If you can't afford to offer a lower price, try different ways to accomplish it. You could find different suppliers, joint venture with other businesses, sell back-end or upsell products to make up for the loss, etc.

Always sell people the rights to reproduce your product. You could sell the rights straight out for one price or collect royalty payments from each sale they make. You could just create one product or idea and sell it to one or more businesses then let them do all the work. All you need to do is collect the money.

Always give your potential customers a bonus that will actually pay for their purchase. It could be money saving coupons, an affiliate program, etc. For example, you could say, "Buy our product for only $47 and get 6 bonuses valued at $250!" Another example would be to say, ""Buy our product for only $47 and just 2 affiliates will pay for it!"

It is important to change the benefits on your product ad from text to links. When people click on the link, it will take them right to the order page. It'll give them an urge to buy your product. People will usually click on links because they think they might be getting one of the benefits for free.

Be sure to charge people a cheap price to get a sample of your product. If they like it, they can pay full price to get the full version. Yes, you could offer a free sample too. When you charge for a sample, it gives your product more perceived value and you end up making a little money at the same time.

Be sure to offer freebies that are related to the product you're selling. It could be free monthly updates, a free ezine, free consulting, etc. Other rarely-used freebies could be an extended guarantee or warranty, a free coupon for some other business' product or free lifetime product replacement.

Always show your prospects a sample page out of your free ebook. Just black out some of the important information. This will make your prospects curious to download your free ebook.

If you sell information products, this strategy can also work from them as well. Use it for your free ezine to gain more subscribers too.

Always provide a low and high priced version of your product. Show benefits of each version side by side. People usually spend a little more for extra benefits and features. When they are side by side, the one with the most benefits usually grabs people's attention quicker too.

Always offer the reprint rights to your free ebook. You can allow people to sell it. Your ad in the ebook will be seen by proven, money-spending customers as well as freebie seekers. You could also provide people with proven ad copy and an ebook cover graphic.

Be sure to make your target audience's experience reading your ad positive. You could educate them, tell a joke to make them laugh or compliment them to make them feel good. If their experience is enjoyable that's all it might take for them to decide to buy your product, subscribe to your free ezine or join your affiliate program. All these actions can lead to income for you.

It is important to redesign your product for specific niches. You can create multiple profits with very little work. For example, you could easily turn a business ebook into an online auction business ebook and auction it off at online auctions. You would have a whole new and related target audience.

A good technique is to give your prospects discount coupons on other products when they purchase your product. It could be your products or other businesses you made deals with. Just contact other related businesses and propose your idea to them. They may do the same for your business too.

Begin publishing an extra issue of your ezine every week. You could charge a recurring monthly subscription for the free subscribers who want to view the extra issue(s) each week. You could also include no ads in the extra issue because you're charging a subscription fee.

Never load your website with a lot of high tech clutter. Your visitors may miss your whole sales message. Haven't you ever visited a website which had graphic ads, text scrolling and flashing words all crammed together? If you have, it was likely you found it confusing and hard on the eyes and you just said 'forget it'.

Never use unnecessary words or phrases on your site. You only have so much time to get your visitor's attention and interest; make every word count. Use short words, phrases, sentences and paragraphs. Also highlight attention-grabbing words like love, money, sex, etc.

Never make the mistake and think that everyone will totally understand your website message. Use descriptive words and examples to get your point across more smoothly. Don't use hard to understand words that they might have to look up in a dictionary because they won't, they'll just leave your website.

Never write your strongest point or benefit only once. You should repeat it at least 3 times because some people may miss it. Also when you repeat something it gets stored in your prospect's brain easier. This may persuade them to buy later on down the road because they will remember it when they really need or want your product.

Never push all your words together on your website. People like to skim; use plenty of headings and sub-headings. People don't have time to search and read through every word. It's also harder to read online than offline. But you could remind them they could print out your web page to read it later when they are offline.

A good technique is to offer your visitors a free ebook if they subscribe to your free ezine. For example, you could say, "Subscribe to our free ezine and get our new ebook for free!" Another example, "Subscribe to our free ezine and get five ebooks with full give-away rights!"

Never use 50 different content formats all over your website. Try to use only one or two of the same fonts, text sizes, text colors, etc. You don't want your visitors getting frustrated because they have to keep refocusing their eyes. Plus it looks unprofessional not to have a consistent look throughout your website.

Always offer easy navigation. People will leave quicker if they have a hard time finding what they're looking for. Don't get them lost or they will leave. You could have a keyword search box, a side, top or bottom navigation bar, a website map, etc.

Never let selling words and phrases go unnoticed. Highlight important words and phrases with color, bolding, italics, underlining, etc. Also think about each and every word you use on your website. Ask yourself "Is this word going to persuade them to buy my product, join my affiliate program, subscribe to my ezine", etc.

Always give people plenty of things to do at your website. Allow them to submit classified ads, play interactive games, add their link, sign your guest book, etc. This will keep them busy and they will have a higher chance of seeing your ad a couple of times and buying your product or service.

Always address your targeted audience on your business site. For example, "Welcome Internet Marketers". If you have more than one, address them all. When you want to get their attention in the ad copy, you could say, "Attention! All Internet marketers, business owners, opportunity seekers and other entrepreneurs."

Be sure your content and graphics are relevant to your website's theme. You wouldn't want to use a bird graphic on a business website, unless the bird had a business suit on or was doing something business related. That would grab your prospects' attention and the bird would convey the impression that you sell to businesses or that you are a business.

Always alert visitors by email when you add new content to your website. This will remind people to revisit your website. For example, you could say on your website, "Sign up to our opt-in list to be reminded in the future when our website is updated or we add new products."

Always offer a way for visitors to contact you on each web page. List your email address, fax number and phone number. If you're selling a product, remind them to order on each page. If you're giving away a free subscription to your ezine, remind them to subscribe on every page.

Be sure to give people the option of viewing your website offline. Offer it by way of an autoresponder message or by a printer-friendly web page. They may forward it to their friends or family members if it's an email or they may give it to them if they have it printed out.

Always make sure that at least 50% of your content is original. The other option is to offer something else original other than content, like software or an online utility. You need to offer something they can't go any- where else to get. Then they can't think, "Well I saw another website that has that same free ebook so I'll just go there instead."

Be sure to offer your visitors incentives for revisiting your website. You could give them new content, ebooks, software, ezines, etc. Offer a new weekly contest so they have to revisit every week to re-enter. Offer a new, original freebie every week so they have to revisit. You can just ask them to sign up to a reminder email list.

Always publish FAQs for your business, products and website. They could have questions about multiple parts of your business. You could answer questions about your products, business, website, free ezine, affiliate program, message board, chat room, free ebook and other services.

Be sure all links on the navigational bar are clickable. If people can't get to where they want to go, they will leave. It's a good idea to go through your whole website and check all your links once in awhile. There are also software programs that can do it for you too.

Always organize your website in a logical and profitable sequence. You don't want to give away a freebie before they learn about the product(s) you're selling. Make your visitors see at least one or two of your ads before they get to your freebie. Then include those ads somewhere in or around your freebie.

Be sure to use plenty of examples in your ad copy. This will allow your whole target audience to understand your sales pitch completely. If they don't understand your product offer, how do you expect them to buy? Have a few younger kids read it. If they understand it, you'll know an older person will definitely understand it.

You can gain extra credibility by using terms your readers may not understand but can follow, by explaining them in simple terms. This will show you're an expert. People often find it interesting to see new words as they could get bored seeing the same old words every day.

Always reveal how excited you are about the product. You could use words, or even a picture of yourself looking very excited. For example, you could say in your ad copy, "I'm super EXCITED about our new product!" Another example, "I'm so PUMPED UP about our new product I can't wait to tell you about it!"

Be sure to write your ezines ad to sound like it is common sense to subscribe. For example, you could say, "Everyone knows you have to know a few things before you start a business!" Another example, "We all know that knowledge is a key factor in making a business profitable."

Always assume people are going to instantly subscribe to your e-ezine. For example, "Dear Healthy Subscriber". They will want to subscribe in order to feel healthy. Another example, "Dear Intelligent Subscriber". They will want to subscribe in order to feel intelligent.

Always allow your subscribers to collect things from each issue of your e-ezine. It could be ebooks or software. They'll tell others and those people will subscribe too. For example, you could say, "In each issue of our e-ezine we will be giving away a new limited edition business report! Collect them all!"

Be sure to tell people what their friends or family might say as a result of them learning what's in your e-ezine. People care about what other people think of them. For example, you could say, "Just imagine your wife telling you how proud she is of you for starting your own business!"

Always make people feel like it's their idea to subscribe, they will be less hesitant. For example, you could say, "You are making a smart decision for subscribing." Another example, "Thank you for making an intelligent choice and subscribing to our e-ezine!" Plus you're assuming ahead of time they are going to subscribe.

Always use less than seven points in your ad copy. If you start revealing too many topics, your readers might get confused and quit reading. Your points could be your benefits, guarantees, testimonials, closing, opening, postscripts, and headline. Some other points would be features, case studies, customer lists, etc.

Chapter 2 – Psychological Triggers

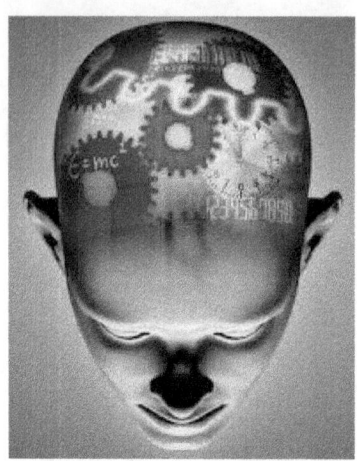

Psychological triggers are defined as triggers that cause a customer to perform a certain action by programming the mind using ad copy. It sounds complicated but it isn't and you are subjected to psychological triggers every day.

One of my associates, Dr. Harry Jay, explains psychological triggers in detail in his book "The Psychology of Sales" http://www.amazon.com/dp/B006IUH0GI

So let's get at it…

It is important to include the reprint/reproduction rights with your product. This increases the perceived value because people can start a business and make money. You can also include some of your advertisements in or on the product. The more it gets resold, the more your ad will be seen.

Be sure to get the word out about your product and brand it. This increases the perceived value because people believe brand name products are better quality. If you want to quickly brand your product, team up with an already branded business and use their name. You could just give them a percentage of your profits.

It is important to participate in chat rooms related to the product you're reselling. Start a conversation with a person without trying to sell to him or her. Later on, while you are chatting, mention the product you're creating a friendship or finding a joint venture partner.

Always create a free ebook with the advertisement and link of your affiliate website. The subject of the free ebook should draw your target audience to down-load it. Also submit it to some ebook directories. The more exposure your free ebook gets, the more your ad will be seen.

It is important to start your own affiliate program directory. Join a large number of affiliate programs and list them all in a directory format on your website. Then just advertise your free affiliate program directory. You will earn commissions and gain sub-affiliates. Plus you could start an affiliate-related ezine too.

Be sure to write your own affiliate program ads. If all the other affiliates use the same ads that you do, it won't give you an edge over your competition. Use a different ad to give yourself an unfair advantage over all the other affiliates. If you have sub-affiliates, tell them to do the same.

Always use a personal endorsement ad. Only use one if you've actually bought the product or service for the affiliate program. Tell people what kinds of benefits are gained when purchasing the product or service in order to write an honest endorsement.

Always advertise the product you're reselling in your signature file. Use an attention-getting headline and a good reason for them to visit your affiliate site. Make sure your sig file doesn't go over 5 lines. Also include your name, occupation, business name and email address.

It is important to join a web ring; just Google "web ring". It should attract the same type of people who would be interested in buying the product you're reselling. You could also trade links on your own with other related websites. Also you could create an ezine ring with other ezine sites.

It is important to participate on web discussion boards. Post your comments, answer other people's questions, and ask your own questions. Include your affiliate text link under each message you post. If they read your message and like it, they may click to see what else you have to offer them.

Always create a free ezine. Use your ezine to advertise the affiliate programs you've joined. Submit your ezine to online ezine directories and promote it on your website. Trade ezine ads with other publishers!

Be sure to start a private website. Use it as a free bonus if people buy the product you resell. You could also allow people to join for free and you could advertise the affiliate program you've joined. You could also charge a subscription fee for an upgraded version of it.

Always provide your website visitors with content they can't read anywhere else. People will stay longer at your website to read the original content. You could also allow them to read through your ezine and archive the back issues on your website. Or you could charge access to the back issues because it would be original content.

Always remind your website visitors they can print out your content. They may browse around your online store while it's printing. They may read it at home, work, outside, etc. Other people might see what they're reading and want to visit your website or subscribe to your ezine.

Always offer your website visitors a freebie if they take the time to fill out your online survey. They'll be at the site longer and might buy something afterwards. Your survey could ask them what kind of products they want, what they think of your customer service, how they like your website, etc.

Always offer your visitors free software that they can download right from your website. While they are waiting they might read your ad. Also, if possible, include your ad in the software so after they open it, they'll see your ad again. This will help increase your sales.

Be sure to provide a huge online directory of information that your visitors could search through. The directory must contain information your visitors would want. It could be news stories, how-to articles, interviews, case studies, profiles, survey results, online audio, online video, ebooks, reports, etc.

Be sure all your web pages load fast or your visitors will get bored and leave. Time is precious; they won't waste it waiting for your site to load. Do not use too many graphics and high tech gizmos. They may have a hard time finding your product ad.

Always tell your visitors what's offered at your website at the very beginning. If people are confused about what's being offered they may leave too early. You could tell them the benefits they get and the things they can do at your website, like subscribe to your ezine, read free articles, download free ebooks, learn to increase their sales, etc.

Be sure your website looks professional. People will get turned off and leave if they see a lot of spelling and grammatical mistakes. You don't want any broken graphics or links either. Make sure your background colors don't make your text hard to read.

A good technique is to hold a holiday sale for your potential customers. For example, you could tell them every-thing on your site is discounted by up to 50% on Thanksgiving Day. Another example, "Fourth Of July Sale! Buy One, Get One Half Off!" Using holiday sales gives you a specific and credible reason for your prices to be lower.

Always use headlines and sub-headlines all over your website that will grab your visitors' attention. They will attract them to explore your website longer. They could be for your free ezine, product ads, free content, message board, chat room, etc.

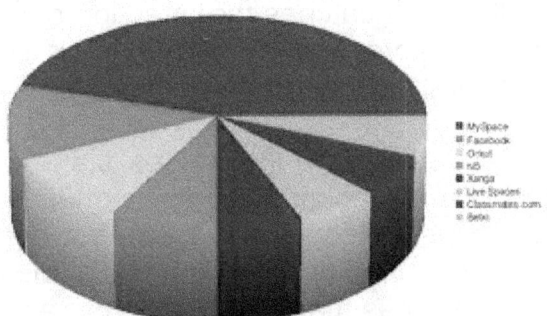

Be sure to place colorful graphs, pie charts and other charts in your ad copy. Use charts as they will grab a person's eye because they are usually colorful. They will also support your product or service claims and allow your target audience to understand them easier - money-back guarantees, testimonials, special offers, discount sales, etc. You could place them in boxes, in front of different colored backgrounds; assemble symbols or graphics around them, etc.

Always use short sentences or sentence fragments in the body of your ad copy. A short burst of words can catch a skimmer's eye with one quick glance. If people have to read a long sentence or paragraph in order to understand your message, the skimmers may not order from you.

Always highlight all the important keywords and phrases in your ad copy. You could use bolding, underlining, different colors, graphic text, italics, symbols, indents and extra spaces to highlight the important words or phrases.

Always place attention-grabbing pictures above and within your ad copy. A powerful technique is to use 'before' and 'after' pictures of people using your product. They will give your target audience a clearer vision of what you're offering. That will help them imagine themselves getting the benefits of your product.

Be sure to use a headline that catches the attention of your of headlines, free offers, guarantees, testimonials, news stories, questions, benefits, warnings, statistics, features.

Always make your ad's keywords and phrases stand out by enlarging the text. This technique works wonders with headlines and sub-headlines. People see them first because it's easier for their eyes to focus on. You could also use different fonts for your headlines than the rest of your ad copy.

Always make your product's list of benefits and features stand out by using a symbol in front of each of them. The symbol could be a dash, solid circle, star, etc. Also indenting them will help make them stand out. Each benefit should be written like a headline to get the readers' attention and tell them what's in it for them.

Chapter 3 – Scarcity and Urgency Triggers

There is no other more powerful psychological force greater than scarcity thought with the human mind! It permeates our consciousness; it dominates our thought patterns. Someone...anyone...is getting our stuff instead of us and this cause all of us to act!!!

The ideas and methods described in this chapter can easily double, or more, the effectiveness of your sales process. Using these psychological triggers you can over clock your sales process and not only give yourself a jumpstart ahead of your competitors but steadily increase your lead.

In today's society of fast paced living that is dominated by consumerism and entertainment, people have had to develop mental shortcuts in order to keep up in all walks of life. With these powerful proven methods you can utilize these shortcuts to funnel the common desires of your prospects straight into your bank account!

In any type of marketing, the power of words is often the best weapon you could possibly have in your sales process.

By using these extremely effective methods of persuasion you can capture the attention of your readers, and then trigger their urge to buy by creating an overwhelming sense of urgency to buy the product. Your prospects won't know what hit them!

How many times have you let your potential customers slip away because they had too much time to second-guess?

How many times have you let your rock solid products and ideas be set aside simply because they weren't deemed as necessity?

Don't do this!

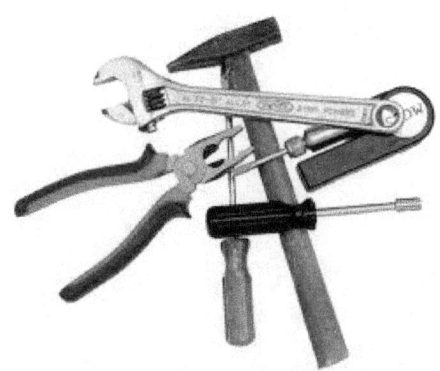

Using the undeniably powerful tools of urgency and scarcity, back them into a corner with their own desires so that they don't have any room for hesitation. You will be utterly amazed with the effectiveness of these tools in practice. With all that said, let's jump right in.

In any type of marketing, the power of words is the cornerstone of any business. It can be your most powerful asset, or your worst enemy. Luckily, with these techniques, they can be surprisingly effective in a way that you never thought possible.

Just by simply changing a few words, or creating a simple emotion or idea, you can trigger subconscious urges in your reader without them even realizing it.

In this book, I will specifically be focusing on urgency and scarcity. These are two extremely effective triggers that should be implemented in virtually every sales process.

Your sales copy is always **the most important part** of your marketing so it is important that you spend time on every aspect of it.

By creating a sense of urgency or scarcity, you are employing one of the most powerful marketing tools and one of the simplest ways to do this is with the power of words.

Key Phrases to Use in Any Sales Process

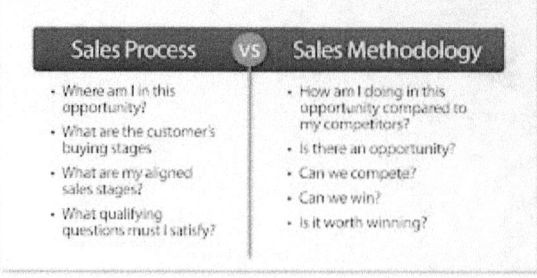

When employing your marketing campaign, it is extremely important that your reader realizes he may never get the chance to own your product again; otherwise he or she may put it off until "later" and never end up ordering. This happens all too often, and it's what we're trying to prevent here.

I want to demonstrate some examples of different phrases you can use to create a real sense of urgency and/or scarcity that will really put pressure on the reader.

• "I reserve the right to change this offer at any time without notice."
• This unbelievable offer will not last much longer because supplies are running dangerously low.
• This incredible program is coming to an end as we are limiting the number of people who join to protect the system. Make a change in your life AND your income before this once in a lifetime opportunity closes its doors for good. This insanely low introductory offer will not last forever! We want loads of people to use our product so we can use their amazing success stories and testimonials ¬then we will raise the price back to the original amount.

A good many direct marketing sites have fine-tuned their marketing process to create a really sense of urgency.

I recommend that you study their sales processes and take note of what phrases they use to increase urgency and scarcity.

A good many of these sales sites can be found at Clickbank.com http://www.clickbank.com. Be sure to look for the products that are selling the most. Take a look at their sales copy and order process and model them.

Right about now, many of you are saying, "I already knew that." Well, are you doing it? Seriously, adding just one of those phrases to your sales copy will pay for this ebook MANY times over.

Hitting Nerves - Know Your Customer

By HikingArtist.com

Any good marketer will always know his target market so well that he could easily identify with them. The better you know your potential prospect the better you will understand their wants, needs, fears and insecurities – the things that make them "tick".

Emotions are universal. Virtually everyone has them to some degree. The number of people who share similar wants, fears, needs etc. is so large that if you can successfully hit one of those nerves, the reaction would be massive. This gives you a lot of leverage.

The average customers might be (just as examples) eager for results, weary of scams and maybe wanting to learn the "advanced stuff". Those would be extremely easy nerves to hit on with urgency and scarcity.

By really knowing your customer, you should be able to also know what makes them tick. Their motivation and desires can be used to drive them to a sale just as easily as their fears and failures.

Always identify an emotion that may easily be triggered by the pressure of urgency or scarcity. If your market is extremely competitive, play off the angle that they might be missing the chance to get ahead of their competitors. "Your competition is already using this and the offer ends soon!"

When your market happens to be product based or service based, "wow" them with the content or quality then pressure them with limited supplies and limited time offers. That way if your prospect is even slightly interested they can justify an impulse buy with the fact that it was their only chance to ever get such a great deal or product. Don't give them time to decide whether or not they actually need it even if they do. They'll get distracted, and leave the grasp of your sales page.

The Exact Wording for Different Situations

By using different urgency and scarcity angles there are certain words that work better than others in order to set off triggers. They can create certain ideas and impulses that are often times very difficult to ignore. When using limited time offers, one time offers, promotions etc. use words and phrases such as:

• "Last chance to chance you life forever!"
• "Once in a lifetime opportunity!"
• "Keep up with your competitors!"

• "Don't get left behind!"
• "Act NOW before it's too late!"
• "This offer will NEVER be available again!"
• "If you order within the next 24 hours..."
• "Only if you order TODAY!"
• "Very limited time offer!"
• "...while it's still available!"
• etc...
You get the idea.

Be sure to drive home the feeling that the opportunity will be gone in a flash and it will leave them in the dust feeling stupid for not jumping on it. For more ideas go back to clickbank.com. It's an excellent place to browse through excellent sales copy. They'll even tell you which ones are the best selling offers.
So what does that mean for you? That means that you can actually see which sales letters are converting and take the guesswork out of your next project or rewrite a low performing sales page.

Headlines

Your headline is REALLY important. It can set the entire pace and theme of your entire sales process. You can even implement urgency or scarcity directly into your headline. If your headline doesn't put across a strong, short, compelling message that is hard to ignore, then many prospects will simply not read your sales page. The tricky thing about headlines is that they need to accomplish so much with such a small amount of words. No one will read your copy if you don't snag them with the headline.

Your headline should be designed to get attention and be persuasive. There are many ways to approach this but these are two main methods that cover most angles. The most common way is to, in as few words as possible, show the reader how they can save, gain or accomplish something that will positively impact their life. This can apply to anything from entertainment or mental stimulation to financial and mental security.

Your headline should point out something negative that the reader can avoid. This can apply to embarrassment, financial mistakes, discomfort or whatever else people want to avoid. You hit on a nerve and give a quick, easy glimpse, or the promise of, a simple solution. You know the phrase you always hear: "The fear of loss is greater than the desire for gain."

Your headline is the only thing that will get people to read your ad. Think in terms of this: your headline should be intriguing, persuasive and urgent enough that it will be more difficult for your reader to NOT read the article.

When you have found your attention getting angle, add a hint of urgency or scarcity so that people are not only interested in reading your sales copy, but they feel it is important to do it quickly. This is the key that makes all the difference.

Call to Action

You could have the most winning sales copy in the world but if you don't ask for action than the majority of the time you will lose your prospect. They may be thinking that the ad was extremely compelling, hard to tear away from, and that the product was interesting, but a call to action is the last step in the sales process that pushes them to buy. Without it, many visitors simply leave, or don't know what to do.

Remember that your sales process should give the reader the incentive to buy. Waiting for the reader to come up with the idea to buy is simply bad advertising. Give the reader a reason to act fast before you lose their attention. There are a few different methods to approach a call to action, but urgency and scarcity are going to be the most effective ways to trigger the urge to buy.

- Give a time limit on your offer so that the prospect knows he must act quickly.
- If your product has a limited supply or it is necessary to act fast in order to get a good selection, make this very clear.
- If the price of your product or service is increasing, give your prospect a date if possible. The idea of loss creates urgency.
- If the price of your product or service is decreasing or has been reduced, pressure your prospect into taking advantage immediately.
- Make sure you emphasize all the benefits your prospect will get for making an immediate purchase.

- Emphasize everything your reader misses out on or loses for every moment he hesitates.
- If your product is guaranteed, be sure to emphasize that fact so that there is no reason for hesitation.

One Time Offer (OTO) Upsell or "Thank You Pages"

There are a good many sales pages that use the same exact templates for their one time offers and upsells and as a result, they are almost invisible. So be creative when you're creating yours. They were extremely effective at first, but after people saw it a million times it started to sound like a joke and people were expecting it.

There are a good many different and newer ways to approach this and people aren't taking advantage them. Here is an example:

http://www.one-time-offers.com/

There isn't any script or anything sophisticated making this one time offer. The best way to use an OTO is right after you have sold a lower priced product. The key is to get your customer to pull out their credit card for a relatively inexpensive product. It can work with any priced product, however the way that we've used it before we like to lead off with a product priced as low as $7 up to $47.

If you are selling a $7 product, then typically you can make an OTO for $27 to $47. If your front end product is $47, you can offer your OTO for $97, $197, or even $297.

There is no official standard operating procedure (SOP), but keep in mind that you can keep upselling your customer as much as you want. ALWAYS have an offer on your "Thank You" pages.

Let's talk about Thank You Pages: Your "Thank You" page is the page where your customers will land after their payment has been approved. What better time than NOW, while their credit card is still in front of them to make another offer to them? If you're not doing this, you are leaving huge sums amount of money on the table.

The most important factor here is urgency!! Urgency is one of the most powerful psychological triggers that can be implemented in your sales process.

By using "urgency" correctly, it can create an almost undeniable urge to make a purchase.

In your typical action movie, there is usually a point in which time is running out and the hero must take more drastic actions in order to resolve the issue. He may do something totally outrageous but with so little time, what choice did he have? This thought process is natural.

The closer a person gets to running out of time, the more a person feels justified in taking whatever action is necessary. Any marketer who doesn't take advantage of that is crazy! Often times the idea of loss is more powerful than the idea of gain.

Always let your prospect know what he/she stands to lose from hesitation or delay. Don't give them time to think about whether or not they should make the purchase. If anything, only give them time to think about what they lose every moment they don't purchase and what they gain from acting immediately.

Be sure to give a reason no matter how petty it may seem. It will make your prospect feel much better about acting impulsively. The reasons can be very small or they can make a lot of sense and be completely valid.

And it doesn't make as much of a difference as you would think. As long as you're giving a reason you're making it easier for them to order.

When the offer is ending soon make sure you stress that your prospect must act immediately because he may never receive this offer again. This may seem like an obvious reason, but it works like magic. If you utilize these methods properly and create a good sense of urgency, simple reasons such as that one will suffice.

Let's Look at Countdown Timers

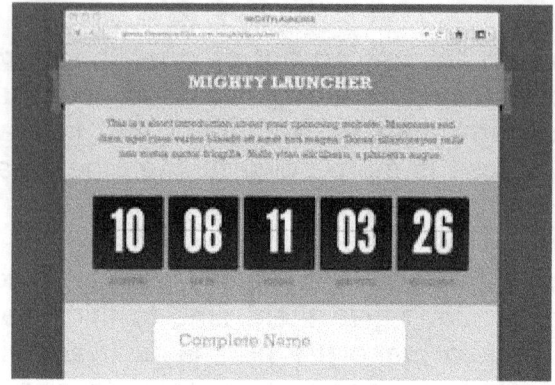

A specific and highly successful way of creating urgency is to have a countdown timer on the sales page. As the window of time gets smaller and smaller the sense of urgency grows. As the sense of urgency grow so does the pressure to act on it.

With a countdown timer, you can boost the effectiveness of your limited time offers or any of your upsell promotions by simply having a visible countdown on the page.

If you have already created urgency correctly with your sales process and given good reasons to validate it, the threat of loss will seem much more real if they can see exactly how little time is left.

The use of countdowns is not only effective for limited time offers and the back end of the sales process. If implemented correctly they can be extremely useful for any type of sales process and even at the front end of a sales page. They can also be highly effective when used on a squeeze page.

The use of countdowns has proven to be excellent marketing tools. It can be a great asset when used with any sales processes. **One important thing you must remember though is that you should always give a reason for the countdown.**

You don't want it to appear like some sort of scam or gimmick. Make sure there is a valid reason no matter how small it may seem.

Here are some examples:

- Offer a fast action bonus so that your prospect actually feels instantly rewarded for jumping on the opportunity.
- If there is a limited amount of your product, stress that fact in order to appear fair.
- Use any little excuse possible such as special events (birthdays, holidays, anniversaries etc)
- Sales are excellent reasons for countdowns even if there is no reason for the sale.

By providing a reason, the countdown will create such a sense of urgency that people will feel justified in acting impulsively. This will help boost your sales dramatically.

Let's talk about the term Nickel Sales. Nickel Sales are basically a variation of the fire sale model. A fire sale, which is an excellent urgency tactic, is a model in which the price of a product starts off at a bargain but increases in price daily. They usually don't last for longer than a few days and the price increases dramatically. It has been extremely successful and it's not hard to see why. It is a perfect example of how urgency and scarcity can drive in sales. If the product was originally $37 on the launch date, then it might be twice as much the next day and so on until the end of the sale. Now, who in their right mind would wait until the last day to purchase something at 3 times the price as the launch date? The incentive to buy immediately is just too strong to resist. Every delay costs them more money.

By using the fire sale, you are using an extremely powerful sales model that can still work very well. Nickel sales are simply slightly different ways of creating a similar sense of urgency. It hits, for the most part, the same nerves and triggers.

Furthermore, with nickel sales, the price doesn't increase by day but by sale. So the product will start off at 5 cents and then go up another 5 cents every time it is purchased.

Nickel Sales is a very powerful urgency tactic that is hard to deny. Every second you wait, the price goes up and someone else has beaten you to the punch. It gives you every incentive to purchase as quickly as possible in order to save yourself some money.

In the customer's mind, the idea of purchasing something at 5 cents is very appealing, especially if you consider the fact that you will be the only person who receives the product at that specific price.

When a prospect is unsure, it will be hard to resist. The urgency created by the idea that everyone else is already buying it, especially your competitors, at a cheaper price than you are paying is enough to justify immediate action.

When the front end price is so affordable, especially if you buy fast, it's easy to get a lot of sign ups so you can make the real money on the back end sales.

The Benefits of Using Promotions, Events and Rollouts

Listed here are some ideas that will help you get going with promotions… use annual holidays, and events and tie them into your sales process.

Examples:

- January – New Years Sale
- February – Super Bowl Sale, Valentine's Day Sale, etc.
- March – St. Patrick's Day, Spring Break, etc.
- April – Easter Sales
- May – Cinco de Mayo (Mexican holiday), Memorial Day Sale, etc.
- June – Summer Blowout Sale
- July – Independence Day Sale
- August – Back to School Sale
- September – Labor Day Sale
- October – Halloween Day Sale
- November – Thanksgiving Day Sale
- December – Christmas Sale

It's obvious that we've targeted holidays. But you want a valid excuse to make the offer. You can also get personal, such as a "birthday" sale, or a "getting married" sale. I've even see some use the excuse that they're moving to a new home or office as a valid reason for a sale. So use your imagination. No rules here but be sure to always have promotions going.

Example Email:

Dear {Mr/Mrs. Customer},

During the busy year we don't always have the chance to thank you for your business. But during {occasion} we would like to do something special to show you how valued and special you really are to us.

So to prove it, I'd like to give you {$xxx} off a {service} this month.

Normally the price for a {service} is {$xxx.xx} but if you call this month -it's only {$xxx.xx}! That's a full {%} off our already low rates. This {services} includes a complete {safety inspection}, {cleaning}, {preventive maintenance}, and {24 point safety check}. Plus, we'll also {perform another minor service} for free at the same time!

But that's not all...

If you're one of the first {50} customers to schedule {this service} done with us, we'll also give you a free {gift with high perceived value}. That's right this {bonus gift} helps you {benefit of gift}...and it's yours absolutely free until we run out of the {50} we recently bought.

So don't wait. If you've been putting off having {your service} done ¬now is the perfect opportunity to save. While this is on your mind, why not give us a call at {your number} to schedule an appointment?

Once again thank you for your continued business this year. I hope you'll be able to take advantage of this special savings during {occasion}.

Sincerely,

{Your Name}

P.S. Remember, if you're one the first {50} customers to schedule an appointment ¬you'll also get a {gift}, absolutely free!

Remember to be creative and use your imagination. There is always a good reason to email, or mail your customers and prospects. Another one of the big psychological triggers that goes hand in hand with urgency is scarcity. It functions in much the same way as urgency. It sets off a trigger in the prospects head by stressing the limit of products or services. This typically increases the value of the product in their eyes.

When the reader is convinced that the product is worthwhile, the idea of scarcity can create an almost frantic urge to buy before it's too late. In fact, that sort of urgency created by scarcity can often be the convincing factor in your copy. You can see examples of the effectiveness of scarcity in everyday life. It doesn't just apply to marketing.

Quite often people realize how much they cared about something only after they couldn't have it anymore. It is so easy to take just about anything for granted that it's hard to tell how much you really want or need something until it is long gone.

When you were hosting a party with thirty people and you announced that there were only a few drinks left it is very likely that you would be trampled by your guests as they stampeded to the drinks. Why not apply this undeniably powerful trigger into your sales process?

There are quite a few ways to utilize the power of scarcity because it has such a huge impact on the minds of your readers. No one wants to be left out of the loop because they waited too long and there was nothing left. Everyone wants to be one of the lucky few who acted quickly and purchased before supplies where exhausted or the offer had ended. Take advantage of them.

The Most Important "Reserve Your Spot" Method

Reserve your spot

By having a limited number of products, this is one way to create urgency through scarcity but it isn't the only one. An excellent method to do this is to create a reserve system in which people can lay claim to a product before it is available. This is an extremely powerful sales model that has yet to be utilized in the online direct marketing niche.

It is difficult to get someone to impulsively commit to a pricey buy. With this model you basically advertise your product before it is available and give your prospects an opportunity to reserve a spot for the product. This doesn't sound like anything new, but the effectiveness comes from the incentives that you provide.

By asking for a small deposit for the reservation and explaining that there will only be 200 packages sold, and they'll sell out quickly.

Getting someone to impulsively put a five dollar down payment on a product is easier than to pay for the whole thing right away.

This technique also guarantees them a spot on the list for a limited product or service. In exchange for their immediate reservation they are promptly rewarded in several ways. Once they have reserved a spot and given the small deposit, immediately send them a free report or download that is only available to people who made a reservation. By making the reservation they are already much more committed to buy.

Another aspect is the fact that the product will also be available to people who have reservations at a slightly earlier time. Let them know that they will have the opportunity to make the full purchase and receive the product 10¬20 minutes earlier than anyone who didn't have a reservation. This will give them the chance to cash in on the fast action bonuses that you will provide.

Be sure to offer fast action bonuses for the first people who purchase. For example: the first 50 purchasers will receive this bonus, the next 100 purchasers will receive this bonus and so on.

By doing this, it will create an overwhelming sense of urgency to reserve and purchase quickly. Not only should there be a limited number of reserve spots, but the faster you buy, the more rewards you get. This is an extremely effective combination of urgency and scarcity.

Be sure that the fast action bonuses are extremely desirable even though their value will be increased by the limited availability. Here are some good examples of bonuses you can offer.

- If available, offer a free teleseminar in which they are coached or advised with an expert.
- Tickets to an event
- Access to a special v.i.p. forum.
- An ebook on a relevant subject
- One-on-one coaching

You can also use a "secret technique" not revealed anywhere else. You can use any bonus that you can think up. This is an excellent fresh sales model that should be utilized as quickly as possible in order to take full advantage. It's a great way to bring something new to the whole "product launch formula" thing that you see all the time.

Promo Codes

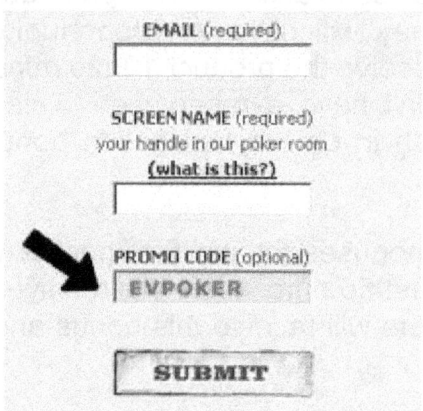

The use of promo codes is an excellent method to create scarcity. If the product or service is in good supply, create a limited number of discounts that act very similar to fast action bonuses.

The use of promo codes is a perfect example of incentive based marketing. Give your prospect an incentive for just about everything.

You provide a promotional code to your customer so that they can enter it into a verification box on the order page. These codes generally provide some sort of discount or benefit that is not available if you don't have the code.

The psychology here is that when someone sees the standard price on the order page and uses the promo code to get it for cheap or even free, it gives them the feeling that they are getting an excellent deal, and increases perceived value. When you give someone something, no matter how small, they generally like you better.

Marketers have been taking advantage of promo codes for a long, long time. It's nothing new.

Just about every marketer gives a free ebook or download or whatever. People just aren't as excited about getting stuff like that. With promo codes you can give all kinds of incentives in different ways that will trigger readers to buy on the front end and back end.

Promo codes are not only excellent incentives; they get the prospect more involved in the sales process. This can lead to a bigger commitment to buy. Just the very act of getting more involved in the marketing process makes the prospect more committed to buy. With a limited number of promo codes being offered prospects will be urged by the scarcity of the promo codes and will rush to be a part of the exclusive deal.

Promo codes can be useful in many different of ways. You can use them as fast action bonuses where only 200 codes will be given out in order to get a huge discount on the standard price. Another application could be to offer a number of promo codes for free in order to get fast testimonials and so on.

Let's Tie In Social Proof with Scarcity

There is another powerful trigger to keep in mind - the power of social proof. The actions and beliefs of others is often an immense influence on the way people make decisions. Not to say that the majority is always correct, but the majority is obviously more influential.

Social proof is, without a doubt most effective when people are unsure about something. When people are unsure about what to believe or how to act they generally look to what everyone else is doing, especially people who are similar to them.

Most people get a large percentage of their information through second hand knowledge. This can be the opinion of experts, which is often times very valuable, or the opinion of the majority.

Take advantage of this fact when trying to urge prospects to buy through methods of scarcity. When a prospect is unsure about whether or not to buy, that is the perfect time to utilize social proof in your sales process.

Stress the fact that everyone in your market is buying the product and it can often make the reader feel more confident about the product.

An excellent way to implement this into your sales process is through specific testimonials. Real life testimonials can be extremely convincing and will add some validity in the eyes of your reader.

By limiting the quantity of your product or service, you want to stress urgency or scarcity and use social proof to prod them into action. Stress that the competition may already own the product and that their time to buy is running out. Provide numbers of people in the same market that have already purchased or experts who support the product. This is seen in advertising all the time; a certain brand of toothpaste is used by thousands of dentists. This triggers confidence in the product so that there will be more reason to buy and less reason to hesitate.

Let's sum it all up...

There is so much competition in just about every market so it is extremely important that you press every advantage that you have. The buyers will rarely just come to you. You have to work for them and push them.

By using psychological triggers of urgency and scarcity, it is such an important part of your sales process and now you have the tools to successfully mold these senses into an overwhelming urge to buy.

It is important to keep in mind that, although these are all excellent strategies, you must use them wisely and when they are the most appropriate.

You can combine them together to create a sense of urgency that your prospect can't ignore, but if you bombard them with too much it can also be a deterrent. Use discretion.

Now that you have learned these "trigger concept" and are armed with the knowledge to effectively drive in sales with urgency and scarcity, use them to make money!

These methods are invaluable tools in your arsenal that, if implemented correctly and strategically, will dramatically increase your sales. While the tips and techniques in this ebook may seem simple, they are very powerful. So take action, implement these techniques today and watch things change in your business literally overnight!

I Have a Special Gift for My Readers

I appreciate my readers for without them I am just another struggling author attempting to make ends meet.

My readers and I have in common a passion for the written word as well as the desire to learn and grow from books.

My special offer to you is a massive ebook library that I have compiled over the years. It contains hundreds of fiction and non-fiction ebooks in Adobe Acrobat PDF format as well as the Greek classics and old literary classics too.

In fact, this library is so massive to completely download the entire library will require over 5 GBs open on your desktop.

Use the link below and scan all of the ebooks in the library. You can select the ebooks you want individually or download the entire library.

The link below does not expire after a given time period so you are free to return for more books rather than clog your desktop. And feel free to give the link to your friends who enjoy reading too.

I thank you for reading my book and hope if you are pleased that you will leave me an honest review so that I can improve my work and or write books that appeal to your interests.

Okay, here is the link…

http://tinyurl.com/special-readers-promo

PS: If you wish to reach me personally for any reason you may simply write to mailto:support@epubwealth.com.

I answer all of my emails so rest assured I will respond.

Meet the Author

Dr. Treat Preston is a behavioral scientist specializing in all types of relationships and associated problems, psychological triggers as applied to commercial advertising and marketing, and energy psychology.

He is also one of the lead research scientists with AppliedMindSciences.com, the mind research unit of Applied Web Info.

He and his wife Cynthia reside in Auburn, California.

Visit some of our company websites
http://appliedmindsciences.com/
http://appliedwebinfo.com/
http://bookbuilderplus.com
http://embarrassingproblemsfix.com/
http://www.epubwealth.com/
http://forensicsnation.com/
http://www.freebiesnation.com/
http://neternatives.com/
http://privacynations.com/
http://survivalnations.com/
http://thebentonkitchen.com
http://theolegions.org

Some Other Books You May Enjoy From ePubWealth.com

21st Century Marketing Genius
http://www.amazon.com/dp/B008A07WBW
Addictions
http://www.amazon.com/dp/B006IGHQD4
Anatomy of Anxiety
http://www.amazon.com/dp/B00777QQYS
Applied Income Model
http://www.amazon.com/dp/B006WZN8M4

Applied Mind Sciences
http://www.amazon.com/dp/B007GK4U08
AWeber Primer
http://www.amazon.com/dp/B00A8G2E3M
A Weapon of Massive Consumption
http://www.amazon.com/dp/B008SUWGZG
A Woman Surrounds A Man
http://www.amazon.com/dp/B008DY2VDO
Be A Prepper
http://www.amazon.com/dp/B007IL5OE6
Be Prepared to Survive
http://www.amazon.com/dp/B007KJ0ANQ
BlueprintCashPro
http://www.amazon.com/dp/B006X0UASS
Blame Me Not
http://www.amazon.com/dp/B008D37AI6
Body Language
http://www.amazon.com/dp/B006INI18G
Body Talk
http://www.amazon.com/dp/B0079MA1XS
Bouncing Back From Adversity to Success
http://www.amazon.com/dp/B008ZSGPRQ
Bully America
http://www.amazon.com/dp/B008EJ6102
Cartoon Psychology
http://www.amazon.com/dp/B006IUHMN4
CashCodePro
http://www.amazon.com/dp/B006WZRCVM
Chasing Shadows
http://www.amazon.com/dp/B008A5ZRW8
Chelation Therapy
http://www.amazon.com/dp/B006J7YZ54
Confessions of a Child Predator
http://www.amazon.com/dp/B007BB97KU
Confessions of a Satanic Worshipper
http://www.amazon.com/dp//B007DR4838
Control Your Dreams
http://www.amazon.com/dp/B0071YN3L6
Cyber-Daters Beware

http://www.amazon.com/dp/B006J9T4NA
Distraction Marketing
http://www.amazon.com/dp/B006IUVBWM
Dropping Off The Grid
http://www.amazon.com/dp/B006JLGKLC
Drop Three Dress Sizes in 30-Days
http://www.amazon.com/dp/B007F7VHZI
Effective Email Advertising
http://www.amazon.com/dp/B006IV2300
Embarrassing Problems Fix - General Problems Vol 1
http://www.amazon.com/dp/B0075LOK3U
Embarrassing Problems Fix - Female Problems Vol 2
http://www.amazon.com/dp/B0075LO7AQ
Embarrassing Problems Fix - Male Problems Vol 3
http://www.amazon.com/dp/B0075LQNF8
Energy Psychology
http://www.amazon.com/dp/B006JOZ7G8
Famous Cartoon Quotations
http://www.amazon.com/dp/B007POZKNQ
Famous Quotations
http://www.amazon.com/dp/B007IRKDM8
Female Wolf Packs
http://www.amazon.com/dp/B006JMHD80
ForensicsNation Bushwhacker Program
http://www.amazon.com/dp/B007I9AHVS
ForensicsNationsStore.com Catalog
http://ForensicsNationStore.com
FreebiesNation Blueprint Program
http://www.amazon.com/dp/B007IFRQ9S
Gender Differences in Advertising
http://www.amazon.com/dp/B006IOCG9U
Getting Rid of Cellulite in 10-Days
http://www.amazon.com/dp/B008XB1A34
How to Write a Kindle Book in Hours
http://www.amazon.com/dp/B008XOY8VC
Howdie Doodie
http://www.amazon.com/dp/B00770WQXA
If It Is Broke; Fix It
http://www.amazon.com/dp/B006JM6NHM

I Have a Mind to Believe
http://www.amazon.com/dp/B006ITGY84
I Know I Am But Who Are You
http://www.amazon.com/dp/B006IOQL7I
In-Image Ads Marketing
http://www.amazon.com/dp/B006X03NBE
Interesting Facts About Left-Handed People
http://www.amazon.com/dp/B00744PXCA
Investment Phrases
http://www.amazon.com/dp/B008LO3Y00
It's All About Database
http://www.amazon.com/dp/B006JO0RBI
Latin Phrases
http://www.amazon.com/dp/B006ITY7TW
Legal Phrases
http://www.amazon.com/dp/B008LOA0Q6
Living Alone
http://www.amazon.com/dp/B0086O1ZC4
Love is the Way
http://www.amazon.com/dp/B006IVYPFG
Male-Female Realities
http://www.amazon.com/dp/B006ITYUNK
Man Up - The Decline and Fall of Manhood
http://www.amazon.com/dp/B006JA2UMG
Massive Traffic Generator
http://www.amazon.com/dp/B006IV1YRS
Men & Women…attract or attack
http://www.amazon.com/dp/B006IU8LU2
Mobile Commerce Blueprint
http://www.amazon.com/dp/B006JO1CX0
Mobile Text Voting
http://www.amazon.com/dp/B006JOI4ZO
Money Is an Effect and Not a Cause
http://www.amazon.com/dp/B008ZGM2MK
Pay Per Call Marketing
http://www.amazon.com/dp/B006XVUD98
Pay Per View Advertising
http://www.amazon.com/dp/B006ZXMI4W
PhattyFat WheytLoss

http://www.amazon.com/dp/B007790O2JW
PLR Cash Tactics
http://www.amazon.com/dp/B006IVGBDU
PrepperNations Blueprint
http://www.amazon.com/dp/B00ARBZNCW
Publish with a Purpose
http://www.amazon.com/dp/B008Z5U4LC
Questions
http://www.amazon.com/dp/B006WQ715S
Real Estate Phrases
http://www.amazon.com/dp/B008LQ7BMK
Satisfaction
http://www.amazon.com/dp/B006JM6ING
Selling Air
http://www.amazon.com/dp/B006JOIS5K
SEONemo ThenSEO
http://www.amazon.com/dp/B006JN54LW
SEONemo NowSEO
http://www.amazon.com/dp/B006JMYHYI
SEONemo SoonSEO
http://www.amazon.com/dp/B006JN5606
SMS Mobile Competitions
http://www.amazon.com/dp/B006JO1MLC
SMS Reverse Auction
http://www.amazon.com/dp/B006JOYKI4
Social Media Marketing
http://www.amazon.com/dp/B006Z7VSGW
Stealing You
http://www.amazon.com/dp/B00778TT6E
Surviving A Financial Crisis
http://www.amazon.com/dp/B007J1QH3C
Surviving YOU
http://www.amazon.com/dp/B007J3M6A8
Teen Idols
http://www.amazon.com/dp/B006IWNPYC
The Color of White
http://www.amazon.com/dp/B008GNIOTM
The Complete Health System
http://www.amazon.com/dp/B006IVHG2K

The Denial of Self
http://www.amazon.com/dp/B008B7OK32
The ePubWealth Program
http://www.amazon.com/dp/B008HHHVO6
The Face of Anorexia
http://www.amazon.com/dp/B007F8M4XG
The Face Of Despair
http://www.amazon.com/dp/B006JPOV2S
The Greatest Fraud the World Has Ever Known
http://www.amazon.com/dp/B008GUBKI2
The Missing Link
http://www.amazon.com/dp/B006WQLNTI
The Other Side of Me
http://www.amazon.com/dp/B006JMYAE0
The Pain Game
http://www.amazon.com/dp/B007DIPZX4
The Perfect Affiliate
http://www.amazon.com/dp/B007RN2T5M
The Postcarders
http://www.amazon.com/dp/B006IUUV6O
The Power of Observation
http://www.amazon.com/dp/B006IU99EY
The Psychology of Sales
http://www.amazon.com/dp/B006IUH0GI
The Science of Psychology EXPOSED
http://www.amazon.com/dp/B007JBR682
The Smack Report
http://www.amazon.com/dp/B007AZIELK
The Story of Stupid
http://www.amazon.com/dp/B007L2QCHK
The Truth About Federal Anti-Hoarding Laws
http://www.amazon.com/dp/B007J4KH4O
The Truth About Snow Skiing
http://www.amazon.com/dp/B0072R1SAU
The Vowel Movement
http://www.amazon.com/dp/B0071NUPZY
To Boldly Go Mobile
http://www.amazon.com/dp/B006JNJTEK
Too Late For Fruit; Too Soon For Flowers

72

http://www.amazon.com/dp/B006IVLXSI
Traffic Jam
http://www.amazon.com/dp/B007SXI0YK
Traffic Media
http://www.amazon.com/dp/B006IUZV28
Video Marketing
http://www.amazon.com/dp/B006XW0J0U
Web Traffic Systems
http://www.amazon.com/dp/B006IVGYAA
What Is It About Yorkies
http://www.amazon.com/dp/B006JMNRQW
Why Men Should Not Be Allowed To Babysit
http://www.amazon.com/dp/B006JMNR6C
Why Women Should Not Use Online Dating Services
http://www.amazon.com/dp/B006J9EMH8
Will I Look Good In This
http://www.amazon.com/dp/B007NCFZ30
Word of Mouth Marketing (WOMM)
http://www.amazon.com/dp/B006X0FXU8
Wordz
http://www.amazon.com/dp/B006IOCSVQ
You Can Run But You Cannot Hide
http://www.amazon.com/dp/B006JLVZC6
You Can't or You Won't
http://www.amazon.com/dp/B007FQ2EJ2

Novels
Common Ground
http://www.amazon.com/dp/B006I5B1YU
Until The Next Time
http://www.amazon.com/dp/B006I7X5JW
No Crimes Beyond Forgiveness
http://www.amazon.com/dp/B006I7WOSA
The Writing of the Wrong
http://www.amazon.com/dp/B006I9FOPI

Religion
BibleBits
http://www.amazon.com/dp/B006ZD702C

Bible Mysteries
http://www.amazon.com/dp/B007J1WZSI
In The Mind of Christ
http://www.amazon.com/dp/B006ZCC8JS
Pastors as Counselors
http://www.amazon.com/dp/B006ZD0I5S
Small Christians
http://www.amazon.com/dp/B008MX216S
The Covenants of the Bible
http://www.amazon.com/dp/B007J3M2GG
The Names of Angels
http://www.amazon.com/dp/B0084S7W9M
The Ten Commitments
http://www.amazon.com/dp/B007LHTR04
Truthful Christianity, Judaism, and Islam
http://www.amazon.com/dp/B007JMIL2G